PITKIN COUNTY
library
inspire growth

PITKIN COUNTY LIBRARY

1

120 North Mill S

D0396212

LC 641.5636 H753   14.95
Holmes, Sandy,
Simply delicious

DOES NOT CIRCULATE

WITHDRAWN

SIMPLY

DELICIOUS

Plant-based recipes for a healthy life.

Sandy Holmes | RDN

Copyright © 2016 SANDY HOLMES

All rights reserved.

ISBN: 978-0-9978405-0-6

DEDICATION

In memory of my
mother, Lucille Saso.
She taught me to cook
healthy meals and inspired
me to pursue my dreams.

ACKNOWLEDGMENTS

Thank you to my family,
friends and clients for
encouragement, recipe testing,
tasting, and the editing
of "the meat" of my book.
This was truly a group effort.

Creative Director | Kelly Alford
Production Design | Hamadou Bocoum
and Caelina Eldred-Thielen
Editing | Linda Sullivan
and Ellen T. Knous

TABLE OF CONTENTS

STARTERS | 11

GLORIOUS GRAINS | 26

SOUPS | 36

MAIN DISHES | 48

STARTERS

You may not be ready to become a vegan or even a vegetarian. Yet, it's hard to deny that Americans eat too much meat, not enough vegetables and too little fiber. We are living longer, but are we healthy while we are living? Most people I know want to eat better, but don't know how to start. This book is for you. This book provides nutritional information, stories and tips to help you move toward better health.

I have been gradually moving toward a plant-based diet since my popcorn and Tab days at Purdue. I have transitioned from pescatarian (a vegetarian that eats fish), to ovo-lactovegetarian (just dairy and eggs), to "cheatin' vegan." Today I would say I'm predominately plant-based. For one, it doesn't carry the same stigma vegan carries and it's true. Occasionally I have eggs and dairy in my diet. I think we strive to do what is right in all aspects of our lives, but we don't have to be perfect. In fact, I think it is almost better if you aren't. Predominately plant-based works for me and it might work for you. Maybe you function better with a bit of fish or dairy. I have to admit, cheese was the hardest thing for me to give up. Even though I realized it was not healthy, it sure tasted good and it was in so many of the ethnic foods I love.

When I first started working at the hospital, I was counseling many of Dr. Morgan's cardiac patients. We spoke on the phone for a while before we finally met. I distinctly remember a conversation in which he was telling me exactly how he wanted his patient to eat.

I said, "Oh Dr. Morgan, you really don't expect your patients to give up cheese forever, do you? I love cheese."

His reply, "You must be a chubby little girl." And I was. It took giving up cheese to move me to a healthy BMI (body mass index).

As a hospital nutritionist, I am often invited to speak locally, and am frequently asked to talk to middle school kids for their health class. I have a presentation for the kids that discusses the benefits of a plant-based diet. After my talk one day, a seventh grade boy raised his hand and said, "I think you are biased." I am biased, but I believe I have the knowledge and the background to support my bias. The more I have studied the whole food plant-based diet, the more I believe it is the optimal way to eat.

One of the things I do as a registered dietitian is to offer reasons for a client to make changes to their diet. I try to explain why they should change the way they have been eating their whole life. We used to teach people a diet regardless of their wishes. Now we work with our clients to figure out how we can help them achieve their nutritional goals. You have a choice. You always did, but now we respect and honor that choice. Just how is your current diet working for you? Be honest.

There are a number of people studying the effects of plant-based diets. Dr. T. Colin Campbell http://nutritionstudies.org (particularly his book, *The China Study*) is the first to influence my life and move me toward my current beliefs. His focus has been on a plant-based diet and the relationship to cancer prevention.

I went on to find Dr. Esselstyn from the Cleveland Clinic and read his book, *Prevent and Reverse Heart Disease*. http://www.dresselstyn.com/site/. Both of these doctors grew up on dairy farms and went through a paradigm shift to be proponents of a plant-based diet. Esselstyn and Campbell created a great documentary: *Forks Over Knives*. It is an introduction to the "whys" of shifting to a plant-based diet.

Dr. Barnard studies a plant-based diet with regard to reversing diabetes. I am talking about type II diabetes (not the autoimmune type). Dr. Barnard started the Physician's Committee for Responsible Medicine http://www.pcrm.org/. Check out his "Vegetarian Tool-kit." I have admiration for Dr. Barnard; he questioned the food guide pyramid and enacted nationwide nutrition changes.

Dr. McDougall http://www.drmcdougall.com/ is working on proving that a whole food plant-based diet can control autoimmune disorders like multiple sclerosis and arthritis.

Dr. Fuhrman http://www.drfuhrman.com concentrates on plant-based diet, weight loss and disease prevention. He also developed the Nutritarian Diet. Although not vegan, it is predominately plant-based. He developed a scoring system for foods that allows you to evaluate them on nutrient density (nutrients compared to calories).

If you want a site that is comprehensive, check out Dr. Michael Greger's http://nutritionfacts.org/. He has spent his life poring over scientific studies. His site has nutrition videos, health topics and a place where you can ask him questions.

These are some of the most famous physicians devoting their lives and practices to plant-based diets, but there are more. The book, *Rethink Food: 100+ Doctors Can't Be Wrong,* lends more support from a variety of different physicians and conditions. The positive side effects from plant-based eating include an increase in cardiovascular condition, weight loss, and energy, and a decrease in cancer risk. Need I say more? I have been in the nutrition field long enough to believe people can find data to support anything they believe in. So, I guess you just have to try it for yourself and see.

Another great resource for a vegetarian lifestyle comes from the Vegetarian Practice Group http://vegetariannutrition.net/. This is a group of dietitians, so I can assure you the information is science-based. The website has a resource tab that discusses things like protein (the subject I get the most questions about). Check out: http://vegetariannutrition.net/docs/Protein-Vegetarian-Nutrition.pdf. They also have great informational handouts on calcium, iron and B12. If you are vegan, you must supplement with B12 as this vitamin is only found in animal foods.

The thing about starters, is you have to start. You can either start by "cliff diving" and giving up everything with a face or a mother, or you can test the waters. For some, often those who have had a significant event (like a heart attack), making a clean cut to go plant-based makes sense. Some argue that it is better to get the taste out of your mouth and re-train your pallet. By the way, your pallet will change. Once you have been following a cleaner diet for a while, you actually will like eating that way. Others have to ease into the lifestyle. You may want to try the baby step approach. Start by incorporating more vegetables and grains into your diet, eating less processed foods or you may want to do "Meatless Mondays" http://www.meatlessmonday.com/.

If you are going vegan this book will give you a good start, about two weeks worth of meals. If you are easing into it, just try one of these recipes from time to time. But, you should have a goal; write it down and tell someone about it. That makes the goal "real" and achievable.

You have the book in your hand, get cooking!

Mushroom Pâté

3 tablespoons vegetable broth
1 onion, chopped
2 cloves garlic, minced
1 teaspoon thyme
1 teaspoon tarragon
1 teaspoon salt
¼ teaspoon pepper
1 pound mushrooms, chopped
1 cup walnuts, toasted
1 15 ounce can white beans, drained
1 teaspoon balsamic vinegar
1 tablespoon sherry

Directions

1. Sauté onion in vegetable broth until soft and translucent.
2. Add garlic, thyme, tarragon, salt and pepper and cook another minute.
3. Add mushrooms and cook 10 minutes, cool slightly.
4. Place mushroom mixture, toasted walnuts, beans, vinegar and sherry into the food processor, mix until smooth. You might have to add a bit of vegetable broth to create a smooth spreadable paste.
5. Chill before serving.

Mushrooms are being studied for their anti-inflammatory, anti-bacterial and possible immune enhancing properties. Mushrooms exposed to or grown in sunlight, are a good source of Vitamin D.

Spicy Carrot Hummus

¼ cup onion, chopped
3 cloves garlic
¾ cup carrots, cooked
4 dried apricots
2 tablespoons tahini
2 teaspoons Dijon mustard
2 tablespoons lemon juice
1 15 ounce can cannellini beans, drained
1 teaspoon salt, optional
2 teaspoons Sriracha hot chili sauce

Directions

1. Sauté onions in their own juices.
2. Steam carrots until tender.
3. Combine remaining ingredients in food processor.
4. Chill.

Perfect for a vegetable dip or a sandwich spread. I use it with a soft corn tortilla, arugula, peppers and onion to make a delicious wrap!

This recipe was inspired after taking my 18th annual hike to Conundrum Hot Springs with my friend, Cynthia. She shared with me her new favorite prepared hummus. I read the ingredient label and here is my version. We've committed to hike the 20 mile round-trip hike annually, even if we need to use a walker.

Muhummara

2 red peppers
1 cup raw walnuts, toasted
3 cloves garlic
2 teaspoons paprika
1 teaspoon cumin
1 teaspoon red pepper flakes
¼ cup lemon juice
½ cup whole wheat bread crumbs
½ teaspoon salt

Directions

1. Cut peppers in half, remove seeds and stems.

2. Roast in a 425° oven for 45 minutes-1 hour.

3. Toast walnuts until golden brown.

4. Put all ingredients in food processor and blend until smooth.

5. Serve with whole grain crackers.

If you get mouth sores from eating walnuts, you might have a slight allergy. Try soaking them in water overnight, before you toast them. Walnuts are a great plant source of omega-3 fatty acid, a good fat.

Baba Ghanoush

1 large eggplant (~1½ pounds)
2 cloves garlic
2 tablespoons tahini
2 tablespoons lemon juice
½ teaspoon cumin
   red pepper flakes to taste
   salt to taste

Directions

1. Cut eggplant in half lengthwise and make 3 lengthwise slashes (don't cut through the skin) in each side of the flesh. Place flesh side down and roast in a 350° oven for 45 minutes until it is soft to the point of collapsing. It will have a wrinkled look.

2. Peel flesh from skin (toss the skin) and place roasted eggplant in food processor.

3. Purée with the remaining ingredients.

4. Refrigerate to blend flavors.

5. Serve with homemade whole wheat pita chips (just buy whole wheat pita bread, cut into triangles and bake in hot oven until crisp).

This has become a staple in my refrigerator. I will sometimes use a dollop of it on a bed of lettuce with some black olives and sliced tomatoes. I like to use it as a dip for carrots and other raw vegetables.

David's Sprouted Bean Salad

    5 cups assorted sprouted beans*
    2 tablespoons balsamic vinegar
    ½ cup red onion, finely chopped
    ½ cup fresh tomato, diced
    1 jalapeño, seeded and chopped fine
    1 clove minced garlic
    ½ teaspoon onion powder
       salt and pepper to taste
    1 avocado, diced

Directions

1. Mix beans, vinegar, onion, tomato, jalapeño, garlic, onion powder, salt and pepper.

2. Stir in avocado just before serving.

This takes a few days of planning to make. The indoor bean garden takes ~2 days for the smaller beans and 3 days for the garbanzo and adzuki. David just mixes the beans all together. I use pint ball jars and put cheesecloth on top, for easy draining. Soak them overnight, rinse them 3 times and drain. Every 24 hours, rinse and drain them again. Once sprouted, they can be stored in the refrigerator until use (but no longer than a few days, a week is pushing it). Sprouted beans are an earthy food. I wouldn't recommend this be the first recipe you try, unless you have been plant-based for a while.

*I use green and black lentils, adzuki, mung and garbanzo beans.

Avocado Corn and Tomato Salad

    2 heirloom tomatoes
    2 avocados
    1 cup fresh corn kernels, about 2 ears of corn
    2 tablespoons lime juice
    3 tablespoons fresh cilantro, optional
      salt and pepper to taste

Directions

1. Dice tomato and avocado (I cut the avocado in half, dice it in the skin and give it a squeeze).

2. Stir in lime juice and corn kernels.

3. Season with salt and pepper and cilantro if desired.

4. Serve on a bed of arugula.

This summer dish needs fresh ingredients. A great way to use up your left over corn-on-the-cob. Go to your local farmer's market to obtain seasonal and tasty ingredients.

Scotty's Balsamic Figs

12 fresh figs
   balsamic vinegar
   honey

Directions

1. Line a cookie sheet with foil or parchment paper.
2. Wash, stem and cut figs lengthwise and place on cookie sheet, skin side down.
3. Place 2-3 drops balsamic vinegar on each fig.
4. Drizzle lightly with honey.
5. Broil 10 minutes, then change to bake at 300° until tender, approximately 20 minutes more.

These are so delicious, but you don't want to eat too many—they are very high in fiber! Scott is my nephew. He and his wife, Stacy have a French restaurant, Chez nous in Humble, Texas. One fall weekend, I picked Scott up from the airport and he told me, "You have 72 hours to fix me." He called my place the "Vegan Ranch." We worked together in the kitchen to find plant-based substitutes for his usual rich foods. Scott told me he needed to take "baby steps." He helped me realize not everyone is able to dive into a whole food plant-based lifestyle. The good side, he has made progress and is happy that wine is plant-based.

SIMPLY DELICIOUS *Plant-based recipes for a healthy life.*

Tofu Lettuce Wraps

- 1 14-16 ounce tub firm block tofu, cut in 1/4" cubes
- 1 cup asparagus, diced
- 1 cup frozen peas and carrots
- 2 tablespoons low sodium tamari
- ⅓ cup catsup
- 1-2 tablespoons Sriracha, to taste
- ¼ cup toasted pine nuts
- 1 tablespoon ginger root, minced
- 2 tablespoons sesame seeds
- 3 cloves garlic, minced
- ½ cup green onions, sliced diagonally
- 1 head butter or bibb lettuce

Directions

1. In a frying pan, simmer tofu in water for 5 minutes and drain.
2. Lightly sauté asparagus with peas and carrots in tamari.
3. Gently mix together: catsup, Sriracha, pine nuts, ginger root, sesame seeds and garlic.
4. Stir in tofu and green onions.
5. Place mixture on a lettuce leaf and fold like a burrito.

I had the opportunity to watch Han, originally from China, make these. I omitted the sesame oil she had used, substituting sesame seeds. I kept the catsup (she assured me it was authentic).

GLORIOUS GRAINS

Grains have been getting a bad rap. Grains were fine until we stripped them of all the nutrients and fiber. We did this to make them last longer on the grocery shelf. Processed foods line our grocery aisles. Whole grains aren't the problem, it is processed grains that should be under scrutiny.

There are health reasons that warrant giving up grains, but I wouldn't advise it if you don't need to. That said, making the switch to whole grains is important.

There is a lot of research looking into the benefits of fiber. Grains contribute fiber and B-vitamins in our diet. We know fiber is important for blood glucose control, provides for regularity, assists in controlling blood level cholesterol, and helps with weight loss.

There are microbes living in your intestines that need to be fed. This is a relatively new area of nutrition and health. I love this article from Web MD "What is Your Gut Telling You": http://www.webmd.com/digestive-disorders/news/20140820/your-gut-bacteria. Vegetable fiber contributes food for your gut bacteria and so does the fiber from grains. There is some thought that those little bacteria, in your gut might be causing you to eat a certain way for their own benefit. You thought you had control of your body?

Grains provide us with carbohydrates. Carbohydrates are our bodies' fuel of choice. Our brain needs them as they are the most efficient energy source. Experimenting with different grains provides for variety. Most grains are easy to prepare and can often be interchanged in recipes.

Farro Salad

½ cup farro
¼ cup champagne vinegar
1 tablespoon honey
1 tablespoon ground flax seed
2 tablespoons orange juice
1 teaspoon salt, optional
¼ teaspoon pepper
⅓ cup dried cranberries
⅓ cup chopped dates (4-5 large dates)
6 ounces mixed greens
¼ cup Marcona almonds, chopped (can substitute slivered almonds)

Directions

1. Wash ½ cup farro in a fine mesh sieve.
2. Place 1½ cups water with ½ cup farro into a saucepan.
3. Cook 25-45 minutes (cooking time depends on the variety of farro). It will be chewy when cooked. If all of the water is not absorbed, drain.
4. Make a dressing out of vinegar, honey, ground flax seed mixed with orange juice, salt and pepper.
5. In a small bowl, combine farro, cranberries and dates.
6. Pour dressing over farro mixture and refrigerate until ready to serve.
7. Toss together greens and farro mixture.
8. Garnish with almonds.

Ground flax seed, high in fiber, also contains the plant form of omega-3 fatty acid. For this recipe, it serves to bind the dressing together and form the "oil" of the vinaigrette. Marcona almonds, from Spain, are softer in texture and a bit more expensive than the California variety.

Mid-East Pilaf

1½ cups onion, chopped
 1 tablespoon sugar
 2 tablespoons white wine vinegar
 3 cloves garlic, minced
1½ teaspoons dried cumin
 4 coriander seeds, crushed
 3 cups water
 ½ cup barley
 ½ cup lentils
 ½ cup brown rice
 ½ teaspoon pepper
 ½ cup raisins

Directions

1. In a 2½ quart saucepan, sauté onion in vinegar and sugar until soft.

2. Stir in herbs and spices and cook 3 minutes or so.

3. Add water and everything except the raisins and simmer about 35-40 minutes until tender.

4. Stir in raisins, cover and simmer an additional 10 minutes until water is almost completely absorbed.

5. Let stand 10 minutes before serving.

Lentils are high in protein and fiber. Because they don't require soaking, they are a great spur-of-the-moment legume choice.

Quick Quinoa Salad

1½ cups cooked quinoa
½ 15 ounce can black beans, drained
½ red pepper, chopped
¼ jalapeño pepper, seeded and chopped fine (optional)
1 fresh mango, peeled and diced (try to keep the mango juice)
½ avocado, chopped (optional)
¼ cup green onion, sliced
2 tablespoons fresh cilantro
¼ teaspoon garlic powder
2 tablespoons prepared salsa
3 tablespoons lemon juice
salt and pepper to taste

Directions

1. Combine all ingredients and mix gently.

With all of my recipes, it is fine to leave out or substitute an ingredient you don't have, don't like, or cannot tolerate. If you don't have lemon juice use something similar like vinegar or another tart juice. If you don't like jalapeño, just leave it out. The first time I made this I had a mango, the second time I had an avocado.

I love the convenience of cilantro in the tube. I find it in the produce section of my grocery store.

Steel Cut Oats

1 cup steel cut oats
1 cup boiling water

Directions

1. Place oats in a pint ball jar.
2. Cover with boiling water.
3. Cool slightly, cover and place in refrigerator overnight.
4. In the morning they will be "cooked."

I never wanted to take the time to make the healthier version of oatmeal, until I tried this method. I reheat mine with 2 dried chopped dates and a tablespoon peanut butter, then top it with 1 tablespoon hemp seed, 1 ounce of almonds, and a serving of fresh fruit.

Clean The Refrigerator Quinoa

2 tablespoons Bragg's Aminos
½ head green cabbage, chopped
4 large kale leaves (stripped from the stem)
1 small onion, chopped
2 cloves garlic, minced
2 purple potatoes, diced
¾ red pepper, diced
1 teaspoon crushed red pepper flakes
½ teaspoon turmeric
   salt to taste
1 cup cooked quinoa

Directions

1. Sauté vegetables in Bragg's Aminos until tender.
2. Add the spices and serve over quinoa.

I love "The Splendid Table" on NPR. My favorite part is when they create a meal from on-hand ingredients. I often find myself doing the same thing in my kitchen. Just about any vegetable can work with this recipe.

Far Out Farro Pesto

½ cup farro, washed and drained
1 cup water
1 cup broccoli, cut into florets
1 cup cauliflower, cut into florets
½ cup carrots, coarsely grated
½ cup mushrooms, sliced
½ onion, chopped fine
3 cloves garlic, minced
2 tablespoons vegetable broth
1 package Simply Organic Pesto Mix
1 14-16 ounce block tofu
½ teaspoon dried oregano
½ teaspoon dried cumin
1 teaspoon paprika
½ teaspoon Sriracha, or other hot sauce
½ cup toasted pine nuts
2 tablespoons black olive tapenade, (or cut up olives if you prefer)

Directions

1. Place farro and water in small saucepan and bring to a boil.
2. Simmer 30 minutes until tender.
3. Drain off excess water.
4. Gently steam broccoli and cauliflower.
5. Sauté onions, garlic and mushrooms in vegetable broth.
6. Prepare pesto using ¼ cup water (follow directions on packet, but use water instead of oil).
7. Press and drain tofu and break into fry pan. Cover with spices including Sriracha and cook until dry (and a little crispy).
8. Toast the pine nuts in a 400° oven (be careful not to burn them).
9. Mix together all ingredients. Serve it hot or cold.

Farro, like barley, can be found in the whole grain variety, semi-pearled or pearled. Use the variety you can find. The more processed it is, the less nutrients and fiber it contains. Farro is an ancient grain from my ancestral country of Italy.

SOUPS

As a skier, I find soups are the perfect ending to a perfect day.

The great thing about soups and most plant-based recipes, is you can make a large batch and freeze them. Good food is important to me, so I cook, but I am living life and not a slave to my kitchen. I believe you can be organized and get a healthy meal on the table even if you are working or playing all day.

Soups are a good way for you to experiment with dried beans, peas and lentils (great sources of protein, iron and fiber). Because I work in a hospital that has an emphasis on orthopedics, I am frequently counseling patients in orthopedic recovery. Dried beans are a perfect food as these patients need all three nutrients to heal.

Puréed soups, like the cauliflower curry, allow those of you more squeamish about vegetables to introduce them into your diet. I have learned from the clients that are new to vegetables, that small pieces are easier to take. I prefer larger "bite-size" vegetables in my soups and stews. The choice is yours...take liberty to make it the way you prefer.

- Remember, you don't need oil to sauté.
- Most recipes can easily be made in a crock pot.
- Soup served with a hearty 100% whole wheat bread is a meal.
- Add herbs and spices in the last part of the cooking process, you don't want to cook these to death.
- You might need a bit more onion, garlic, herbs and spices to make up for the flavor that you are missing from fat. You can never have too much garlic! Okay, maybe some of you might feel I use too much garlic. Remember I am Italian.

Chili Sin Carne

¼ cup onion, chopped
2 cloves garlic, minced
2 tablespoons vegetable broth
2 cups zucchini, chopped
1 cup carrots, chopped
1 28 ounce can diced tomatoes
1 14 ounce can whole tomatoes
1 15 ounce can kidney beans (undrained)
2 15 ounce cans kidney beans (drained)
2 tablespoons chili powder
¼ teaspoon basil
¼ teaspoon oregano
¼ teaspoon cumin

Directions

1. In a large pot, sauté onion and garlic in broth until soft.
2. Stir in zucchini and carrots and cook over medium heat (about 1 minute) stirring occasionally.
3. Stir in tomatoes and kidney beans and bring to a boil.
4. Simmer 30-45 minutes.
5. Mix in herbs and simmer an additional 5-10 minutes.

This recipe calls for minimally processed foods (canned beans and tomatoes). If you are concerned about the sodium (salt) in your diet, use the low sodium products. You can add mushrooms, peppers and hot sauce if you like.

Ellen served this hearty soup when we stayed at her house or "albergues," when we did a "pilgrimage" from Gypsum to Basalt in preparation for the El Camino in Spain.

Wild Rice and Mushroom Soup

1 cup dried mushrooms
2 cups boiling water
½ onion, chopped
3 tablespoons vegetable broth
2 cloves garlic, minced
½ cup wild rice
½ cup brown rice
2 quarts vegetable broth
2 teaspoons herbs de provence
  salt and pepper, to taste
2 tablespoons sherry
½ cup unsweetened unflavored soy milk
  nutritional yeast, as desired

Directions

1. Re-hydrate dried mushrooms with boiling water, set aside for 30 minutes or longer.

2. Sauté onion in 3 tablespoons vegetable broth until soft.

3. Add garlic, rice, mushrooms and the remaining broth—cook until wild rice "opens," about 30-45 minutes.

4. Add herbs, sherry and soy milk and stir constantly to heat.

5. Sprinkle with nutritional yeast.

Wild rice is really a "grass." It is high in both fiber and protein. One of my students pointed out that wild rice has more protein than quinoa. It is always good to have students in class that can teach you something new.

Indian Spiced Carrot Soup

1 teaspoon coriander seed
½ teaspoon mustard seed
½ teaspoon curry powder
1 tablespoon fresh ginger, minced
2 cups onions, chopped
4 large carrots, sliced
6 cups vegetable broth
2 teaspoons lime juice
  salt and pepper to taste

Directions

1. Grind coriander and mustard seed, add curry powder. Put in non-stick saucepan and heat (medium high) for 1 minute. (This releases the flavor).

2. Add ginger and heat stirring constantly.

3. Add onions, carrots and vegetable broth, reduce heat and simmer uncovered until carrots are tender, about 30 minutes.

4. Cool slightly.

5. Purée in blender until smooth.

6. Return to pot, reheat, stir in lime juice and season with salt and pepper.

Ginger is being studied for its anti-inflammatory and pain relief qualities. It also just tastes good! You can peel and slice ginger, and store in the freezer for months.

Thai Curry Cauliflower Soup

½ onion, chopped
2 cloves garlic, minced
1 quart vegetable broth
1 head cauliflower, cut in bite size pieces
2 small red potatoes, diced
½ 14 ounce can lite coconut milk*
2 tablespoons red curry paste
2 tablespoons lime juice
½ teaspoon salt
2 green onions, sliced for garnish

Directions

1. Sauté onion in a small amount of vegetable broth, until soft.
2. Add garlic, cauliflower and potato with remaining broth and cook until potato and cauliflower are tender.
3. Remove from heat and cool.
4. Place in blender to make a smooth consistency.
5. Return to pan, add the coconut milk, red curry paste, salt and lime juice.
6. Heat gently to desired temperature.
7. Garnish with green onion.

Even "lite" coconut milk is high in fat. If you are wanting to make this more heart healthy, use almond or soy milk with ½ teaspoon coconut extract to flavor.

Skiing on Snowmass Mountain, we stopped in for lunch at Elk Camp Restaurant. This is my version of their curried cauliflower soup.

*Freeze the other half of the can of coconut milk for next time.

Pumpkin Lentil Soup

1 onion, chopped
4 cloves garlic, minced
3 stalks celery, chopped
3 carrots, chopped
2 cups red lentils, dry
2 quarts vegetable broth
1 29 ounce can pumpkin
¼ teaspoon marjoram
½ teaspoon cumin
¼ teaspoon pepper
½ teaspoon salt
   hot sauce to taste

Directions

1. Combine onion, garlic, celery, carrots, lentils and broth in a soup pot.

2. Bring to boil, then lower heat and simmer, covered, 30 minutes.

3. Add pumpkin, marjoram, cumin, pepper and salt. Bring to boil.

4. Add your favorite hot sauce (I like Sriracha).

Red lentils are a bit easier to digest than the more commonly used brown ones. They also have better eye appeal.

Gazpacho

    2 ears fresh corn kernels (cooked)
    2 pounds fresh garden tomatoes, chopped
    1 red onion, finely chopped
  2-3 cloves garlic, minced
    1 cucumber, chopped
    1 zucchini, chopped
    1 green pepper, chopped
    ½ cup salsa
    1 28 ounce can crushed tomatoes
    ¼ cup red wine vinegar
    2 tablespoons fresh basil, chopped
  1-2 avocado, diced
    1 8 ounce can low sodium vegetable juice

Directions

1. Mix together and refrigerate until ready to serve.

Took a mid-day hike up Buttermilk, followed by a tailgate at Tiehack with my friend Tierney. I brought gazpacho. Exercise, connection and good food to fuel our healthy bodies.

Sandy's Chili Lentil Soup

1 pound lentils
water, to cover lentils
1 28.5 ounce can tomatoes
1 10 ounce can Rotel tomatoes
1 quart water
1 red pepper, chopped
1 onion, chopped
1 bay leaf
2 teaspoons garlic powder
2 teaspoons basil
1 tablespoon cumin
2 tablespoons chili powder
½ teaspoon cayenne pepper
3 tablespoons tamari

Directions

1. Cook lentils in water until soft, approximately 30 minutes, no need to drain.

2. Add canned tomato products, water and remaining ingredients.

3. Bring to a boil and simmer to blend spices.

4. Add more water to reach desired consistency.

5. Adjust seasonings to your taste.

This recipe is an adaptation of a recipe my mom sent me from the Chicago Tribune. The clipping has followed me for over 30 years.

Tomato Basil Soup

1 quart vegetable broth
3 cloves garlic, minced
3 14.5 ounce cans diced tomatoes
2 cups fresh basil, thinly sliced
   nutritional yeast, as desired

Directions

1. Put vegetable broth, garlic and tomatoes into a 2½ quart saucepan.

2. Simmer over medium heat for about 20 minutes.

3. Add basil, reserving a few leaves for garnish.

4. With an immersion blender, blend soup until puréed. You can also use a regular blender, just be careful not to burn yourself.

5. Garnish with fresh basil and a couple shakes of nutritional yeast.

Processing tomato products enables the phytochemical lycopene to become bioavailable. Although lycopene has been studied with regard to prostate health, no conclusive evidence exists at this time.

MAIN DISHES

People always ask me how I get my protein. If you eat a well balanced plant-based diet, it is easy to obtain adequate protein. Everybody is skeptical, so let me show you how easy it is. The current recommended protein intake is .8 gm/kg. To do a simple calculation, take your weight and divide by two; that number is a little over the minimum grams of protein you need per day. Take a minute and calculate your needs.

Now that you have determined the grams of protein you need, look below as I have provided the approximate protein content of various foods:

Rice, pasta, other grains	½ cup	3 grams
Dried beans, peas, lentils	½ cup	7 grams
Nuts and seeds	2 tablespoons	4 grams
Soy Milk	1 cup	7 grams
Vegetables	½ cup	3 grams
Cereal	1 cup	6 grams
Bread	1 slice	3 grams

As you can see, just about everything except fruits, fats and alcohol contributes protein to our diets. Most plant proteins are not complete proteins. That is because they are lacking one or more of the essential amino acids. In the past, we thought that we needed to combine plant proteins at the same meal. Now we believe we can store amino acids to make the proteins our body needs. Unless you have illness, injury or you are not eating a healthy diet, it is rare to need protein supplementation.

Black Bean Enchilada Casserole

  1 large onion, chopped
  2 green peppers, chopped
  1 14.5 ounce can diced tomatoes
 ¾ cup picante sauce
  2 cloves minced garlic
  2 teaspoons cumin
  2 15 ounce cans black beans, drained
10 corn tortillas
  2 fresh tomatoes, chopped
  1 small can sliced olives
  1 bunch green onions, sliced
  2 cups shredded lettuce
     homemade guacamole* garnish, optional

Directions

1. In a large fry pan sauté onion, green pepper, tomatoes, picante sauce, garlic and cumin.

2. Bring to boil, reduce heat and simmer, uncovered, for 10 minutes.

3. Stir in beans.

4. In a 13x9x2" baking dish layer: ⅓ beans, covered by 5 tortillas.

5. Add ⅓ bean mixture, cover with 5 more tortillas and top with remaining bean mixture.

6. Bake covered in a 350° oven for 30 minutes.

7. Serve with tomatoes, olives, green onions and shredded lettuce.

*I mix 1 diced avocado with 2 tablespoons picante sauce to make a fresh and easy guacamole.

Veggie Paella

1½ cups Arborio rice
3 cups vegetable broth
½ cup frozen peas
½ cup fresh green beans
½ cup orange or red pepper, chopped
½ onion, chopped
3 cloves garlic, minced
4 ounces mushrooms, sliced
3 roma tomatoes, chopped
½ cup zucchini, cubed
1 teaspoon saffron
½ teaspoon turmeric
1 teaspoon salt
1 teaspoon paprika
¼ teaspoon black pepper
2 tablespoons lemon juice

Directions

1. Sauté onion in 2 tablespoons vegetable broth until soft.
2. Add garlic and cook additional 5 minutes.
3. Stir in rice and add remaining broth and vegetables, and cook over low heat stirring frequently.
4. Add spices and continue to cook until liquid is absorbed. Stir often.
5. Stir in lemon juice.

Arborio rice has a higher glycemic index than brown rice. To make this healthier, use brown rice which adds more fiber. This is one of many recipes calling for 3 cloves of garlic. Remember I'm Italian.

Sweet Potato Peanut Stew

2 onions, chopped
2 cloves garlic, minced
2 red peppers, cut in medium size pieces
1 tablespoon brown sugar
1 teaspoon fresh ginger, minced
1 teaspoon cumin
1 teaspoon cinnamon
½ teaspoon cayenne pepper
½ cup fresh ground peanut butter
2 sweet potatoes, cubed
1 15 ounce can kidney beans, drained
1 15 ounce can diced tomatoes
3 cups vegetable broth
1 teaspoon salt
1 cup dry roasted peanuts
  fresh cilantro, as desired for garnish

Directions

1. Heat 3 tablespoons water in saucepan. Add onions and garlic, sauté until softened, about 5 minutes.
2. Add red pepper and cook additional 5 minutes.
3. Stir in brown sugar, ginger, cumin, cinnamon and cayenne.
4. Thin peanut butter with ½ cup water and add to stew.
5. Add sweet potatoes, kidney beans and tomatoes.
6. Stir in vegetable broth, bring to a boil and simmer about 30 minutes.
7. Season with salt, if needed.
8. Serve over brown rice, quinoa, whole wheat couscous or fresh greens.
9. Garnish with peanuts and cilantro.

Dry roasted peanuts remind me of my dad. He loved peanuts, and we both sold them for the Kiwanis Club.

Fresh and Tasty Avocado Boats

  2 tablespoons lemon juice
  1 tablespoon real maple syrup
  1 tablespoon Dijon mustard
  ½ teaspoon dried cumin
  1 teaspoon dried basil
  1 teaspoon fresh cilantro (optional)
  ½ cup cucumber, chopped
  ½ fresh red pepper, chopped
  1 ear corn kernels, cut from cob
7.5 ounces canned black beans (½ can drained)
  3 avocados

Directions

1. Mix lemon juice, maple syrup, Dijon mustard, cumin, basil and cilantro in a small bowl.

2. Add cucumber, red pepper, corn, black beans to dressing and mix.

3. Cut avocados in half and remove the pit. Without removing the avocado from the skin, slice it into squares, by running your knife gently into flesh.

4. Stuff avocado skins with vegetable filling and serve.

Nice for a luncheon on a hot summer day. I didn't always like avocado. This is a food I actually trained myself to like. I ate little bits of it several times and it worked! It is now rare for me not to have an avocado in the house. Store them on the counter until ripe, then transfer to the refrigerator until you want to use them.

Simple Spaghetti Squash

- 1 spaghetti squash, roasted
- 1 onion, chopped
- 8 ounces mushrooms, sliced
- 2 cloves garlic, minced
- ½ cup olives, chopped
- 1 jar spaghetti sauce, no added oil
  nutritional yeast, approximately 2 tablespoons
  red pepper flakes

Directions

1. Roast spaghetti squash in 350° oven until tender, about 1 hour.

2. Meanwhile, sauté onion and mushrooms in own juices.

3. Add olives and garlic and cook 5 minutes more.

4. Stir in spaghetti sauce and heat.

5. Use fork to scrape out squash.

6. Mix all together and put back into the shell.

7. Sprinkle with nutritional yeast and red pepper flakes as desired.

Perfect alternative to a regular pasta dish. Simple, real and delicious! To roast squash: cut it lengthwise and scoop out the seeds. Place skin side up in a roasting pan with a small amount of water. Spaghetti squash and winter squash can be roasted whole and the seeds removed later (if cutting the squash is too difficult).

Stuffed Peppers

1 cup quinoa
2 cups water
4 large green peppers, cut off tops and remove membranes and seeds
1 onion, chopped
¼ cup grated carrots
8 ounces mushrooms, sliced
1 28 ounce can diced tomatoes
2 cloves garlic, minced
12 ounces salsa
2 tablespoons dry sherry
   salt and pepper to taste
1 teaspoon dried oregano
1 teaspoon dried basil
   red pepper flakes, optional

Directions

1. Preheat oven to 325°.
2. Bring quinoa and water to a boil. Reduce to simmer and cook covered until all the water is absorbed (10-15 minutes).
3. In a large skillet, sauté onions, shredded carrots and mushrooms in a small amount of the juice from your tomatoes.
4. Add the tomatoes, garlic and salsa. Cook over medium heat 10 minutes.
5. Add the sherry and cook 10 minutes more.
6. Add salt, pepper, oregano and basil, stir and simmer 2-3 minutes more.
7. Drain the tomato mixture, reserving the liquid.
8. Fold quinoa into tomato mixture. Place peppers in a baking dish and fill with mixture.
9. Add reserved liquid to remaining tomato mixture and pour around peppers.
10. Bake, lightly covered for approximately 55-60 minutes.

Quinoa is a high fiber and a high protein grain. It is prepared similar to rice. Make extra and have it on hand for a healthy side dish. I heard second hand, from a good source (an old Italian lady that cooked for Mussolini) that tomatoes get sweeter the following day.

Crock Pot Garbanzo Bean Curry

1½ cups chopped onion
1 cup carrots, sliced
1 tablespoon curry powder
1 teaspoon brown sugar
1 teaspoon fresh ginger, minced
2 teaspoons garlic, minced
1 Serrano chile, seeded and chopped (optional as this is hot)
2 cans garbanzo beans, drained
3 red potatoes, cubed
1 green pepper, diced
½ teaspoon salt
¼ teaspoon black pepper
⅛ teaspoon cayenne pepper
1 14.5 ounce can diced tomatoes, undrained
14 ounces vegetable broth
2 teaspoons green curry paste
1 cup lite coconut milk
4 cups baby spinach
1 cup frozen green peas
6 lemon wedges

Directions

1. Sauté onion and carrot in own juices over medium heat 5 minutes.
2. Add curry powder, brown sugar, ginger, garlic and Serrano chili, stir until well blended.
3. Place mixture in a 4-quart crock pot and add the next 8 ingredients.
   Cover and cook on low setting for 6 hours until vegetables are tender.
4. Add the curry paste, coconut milk, spinach and peas.
   Cook until spinach is wilted.
5. Squeeze lemon on curry and serve.

Although the number of ingredients in this might scare you, it is really easy to put together. This recipe makes a lot, and it freezes well.

Wraps and Sandwiches

Choose one of the following:

100% whole grain tortilla
Collard green leaf, parboiled with stem gently removed (don't cut through)
2 slices 100% whole grain bread
Bibb lettuce leaf

Spread with one of the following dips

2 tablespoons (recipes in starter section):

Mushroom pâté
Baba Ghanoush
Spicy Carrot Hummus
Muhummara

Top with diced vegetables

½ cup choose what is on hand or as desired:

Tomato
Peppers
Carrots
Broccoli
Green onion
Radishes
Jicama
Sprouts
Olives
Nuts
Seeds
Beans
Spinach

Wrap and eat!

Cynthia's One Pot Pasta

1 box whole grain pasta
2 15 ounce cans diced tomatoes
1 large onion, julienne strips
4 cloves garlic, thinly sliced
1 teaspoon basil
5 cups vegetable broth
1 teaspoon red pepper flakes
4 teaspoons oregano
3 cups assorted vegetables*
   nutritional yeast

Directions

1. Place pasta, tomatoes, onion, garlic and basil in a large stock pot.
2. Cover with vegetable broth and sprinkle with pepper flakes and oregano.
3. Cover pot and bring to a boil.
4. Reduce to low simmer and keep covered for about 10 minutes, stir every 2 minutes or so.
5. Add zucchini, mushrooms, spinach, peppers or other vegetables as desired. Cook until almost all the liquid is absorbed and pasta is tender.
6. Season with salt and pepper.
7. Garnish with nutritional yeast if desired.

A quick-to-fix dinner. Perfect for after a long day at work, or in my case, a powder day!

* Suggested vegetables: zucchini, mushrooms, carrots, spinach and peppers.

Veggie Chili Stew

1 cup onion, chopped
3 cloves garlic, minced
2 tablespoons vegetable broth
½ cup green pepper, chopped
2 14.5 ounce cans diced tomatoes
2 cups zucchini, chopped
2 cups broccoli, chopped
8 ounces mushrooms, sliced
1 15 ounce can kidney beans
1 tablespoon chili powder
1 teaspoon salt
¼ teaspoon pepper

Directions

1. Sauté onion and garlic in vegetable broth until soft.

2. Stir in remaining ingredients and simmer about 10 minutes until broccoli is tender.

Broccoli should always be cooked uncovered to preserve its bright green color.

Tofu Lasagna

8 ounces mushrooms, sliced
1 onion, chopped
3 cloves garlic, minced
3 tablespoons basil
½ teaspoon salt
¼ teaspoon pepper
28 ounce can diced tomatoes
½ cup dry red wine
1 cup fresh basil
10 ounces fresh spinach, steamed gently and drained
3 more cloves garlic
1 14-16 ounce cake firm tofu frozen and thawed, crumbled
1 14-16 ounce cake firm tofu
1 teaspoon salt
½ teaspoon red pepper flakes
12 ounces brown rice lasagna, cooked

Directions

1. In a saucepan sweat mushrooms over medium heat (cook without liquid as they create their own moisture) and sauté until golden brown.

2. Add the onion and garlic and continue cooking until tender.

3. Stir in 3 tablespoons basil, salt, pepper, tomatoes and wine.

4. Simmer and set aside. (Sauce has quite a bit of liquid.)

5. In food processor, combine until blended: 1 cup fresh basil, cooked spinach, garlic, firm tofu, salt and pepper flakes. (Keep the frozen thawed tofu for later.)

6. In a 9X13" lasagna pan layer in this order: 1½ cups sauce, lasagna noodles, green tofu mixture, topped with crumbled tofu. Repeat. Top layer should be sauce.

7. Bake in 350° oven covered with foil, for 45 minutes.

After teaching my class, "Leaning Toward a Plant-Based Diet," several employees at Aspen Valley Hospital requested more vegan options for our cafeteria menu. This recipe is as popular as the meat and cheese version!

Avocado Pesto Pasta

8 ounces whole grain pasta
1 head cauliflower, cut up
1 bunch fresh basil leaves (2 tablespoons dry)
⅓ cup pine nuts, toasted*
2 avocados
3 tablespoons lemon juice
3 cloves garlic
¼ cup sun dried tomatoes
   salt and pepper to taste
   nutritional yeast (optional)
   red pepper flakes (optional)

Directions

1. In a large pot, bring water to a boil.
2. Add pasta and cauliflower and cook until tender.
3. In a food processor, blend the remaining ingredients.
4. Drain the pasta/cauliflower and toss with avocado pesto.
5. Top with nutritional yeast.
6. This is not a saucy dish, it has a macaroni and cheese consistency.

Nutritional yeast is fortified with B12 (the only nutrient you cannot obtain from plant foods). Use it like you would use parmesan cheese. Try it on popcorn! The movie theatre in Carbondale, Colorado has nutritional yeast available for their popcorn.

*I burn these expensive nuts if I don't watch them carefully. So... I toast ¼-½ cup at a time and put the leftovers in a small jar and keep them handy in the refrigerator door.

Kale Pesto Pasta

1 bunch kale
1 box whole grain pasta
1 cup walnuts, toasted
3 cloves garlic
¼ cup lemon juice
1 ounce fresh basil
1 teaspoon dried basil
1 tablespoon nutritional yeast
6 olives, sliced
1 pound mushrooms
  salt to taste

Directions

1. Use the leaves from the kale and cook about 15 minutes, until tender.

2. Cook pasta as directed.

3. Combine cooked kale, walnuts, garlic, lemon juice, basil and nutritional yeast in a food processor, adding water as needed to make a smooth consistency.

4. Sauté mushrooms in a non-stick pan until browned.

5. Pour the kale pesto over pasta and add the mushrooms.

6. Garnish with olives and add salt if needed.

This recipe is a cheaper and more nutritious version of pesto. It is a perfect way for people who are "scared" of kale, to incorporate it into their diet. The walnuts provide a plant form of omega-3 fatty acid (the good fat).

GREENS

So much of our relationship with food is spent trying to avoid foods we are told are "bad" for us. If you haven't figured it out by now, I am a proponent of increasing the vegetables in your diet. Green leafy vegetables and beets have research to indicate they help keep our cells (especially endothelial lining) healthy. They provide nitric oxide (a good guy for your health). Grandma might not have known the mechanism for health that vegetables provide, but now we have the proof. Beet juice is being studied in sports nutrition. Studies demonstrate increased performance, shorter recovery times, and athletes report an easier time breathing. Kale and other green leafy vegetables are being touted by Dr. Esselstyn for improved cardiovascular health. I hesitate to be one of those sensationalist nutritionists, but I believe vegetables are the fountain of youth.

How to make kale tender:

1. Strip the leaves from the stem
2. Cut in tiny pieces
3. Squeeze a lemon onto the leaves
4. Shake on some salt
5. Massage the salt and lemon into the kale
6. Rinse and dry the leaves.

It may be tempting to just drink your kale, but Dr. Esselstyn emphasizes that chewing is an important step in making the nutrients available. Digestive enzymes in your saliva need time to mix with the vegetable matter allowing for better absorption.

There is also study in the area of synergy. Eating a variety of vegetables together may improve absorption and metabolism of nutrients. This is especially true with fats and fat soluble vitamins. The carotenoids in carrots may benefit from a fat source like avocado or nuts and seeds consumed at the same time. There might be something to combining foods, it could be different from what was originally thought.

One last thing on the subject of "green." By eating less animals and animal products, you are lowering your carbon footprint. What is good for you is good for the environment.

Jicama and Carrot Citrus Slaw

3 tablespoons lime juice
¼ cup fresh squeezed orange juice
1 tablespoon sugar
1 teaspoon salt
2 tablespoons cilantro
2 cups jicama, peeled and sliced into matchsticks
1 cup carrots, coarsely shredded
½ red onion, thinly sliced

Directions

1. Mix juices, sugar, salt and cilantro.

2. Pour over jicama, carrots and onions, toss and serve.

Jicama is a white crunchy root vegetable that is high in fiber and low in carbohydrates. It is the perfect vegetable to take on a hike as it is moist and crunchy!

Swiss Chard

6-8 large leaves Swiss chard
  2 tablespoons cilantro paste*

Directions

1. Wash the Swiss chard and strip the leaves from the stem.
2. Cut off the ends of the stem and make lengthwise cuts to allow you to very finely chop (like you would celery).
3. Place the chopped stems into a non-stick frying pan, add wet leaves torn into large pieces.
4. Cover and steam with just the water from the wet leaves at a very low temperature for 30 minutes or so. Check and add tiny bits of water as necessary to keep it from sticking to the pan.
5. Stir in cilantro and heat to blend flavor.

Swiss chard can be purchased in a variety of colors. It is best when very fresh. Swiss chard is one of my mother's favorite vegetables, I am only sorry she is not alive to see me enjoy it regularly.

*I buy cilantro paste in a tube, it lasts longer than the fresh bunch and is a lot less work.

1 cup sweet potato, cubed or sliced into 1/8 to 1/4 inch slices
¼ teaspoon onion powder
⅛ teaspoon cayenne pepper, optional
½ teaspoon salt
¼ teaspoon cinnamon
1 clove garlic, minced
¼ cup Dijon mustard
2 tablespoons Sriracha
1 tablespoon real maple syrup
⅓ cup pecans, chopped and toasted

Directions

1. Preheat oven to 350°.

2. Place sweet potato cubes in a 9X13" baking dish. Sprinkle with onion powder, cayenne, salt and cinnamon.

3. Make a sauce out of minced garlic, Dijon mustard, Sriracha and maple syrup. Drizzle over sweet potatoes and stir to coat.

4. Cover and bake for 45 minutes until tender.

5. Sprinkle with toasted pecans and serve.

Perfect for Thanksgiving!

Elegant Spinach Mold

  2 10 oz boxes chopped frozen spinach
  1 tablespoon ground flax seed
  3 tablespoons warm water
 14 ounces silken tofu
  1 small onion, cut in pieces
  1 cup celery, finely chopped
  1 cup whole wheat bread crumbs
  1 tablespoon lemon juice
  2 tablespoons Dijon mustard
     salt and pepper, to taste

Directions

1. Steam and drain spinach.

2. Mix ground flax seed with warm water until it forms a paste.

3. In a food processor mix onion with tofu until smooth.

4. Put all ingredients into a bowl and mix thoroughly.

5. Put in lightly oiled mold pan. Place mold pan in water bath and bake at 350° for 35-40 minutes.

Blending spinach increases the bioavailability of carotenoids—that just means our body can absorb them better. Lemon juice helps with the absorption of iron. This recipe is a makeover of my family's traditional Thanksgiving spinach dish. I always looked forward to cold leftovers.

½ cup white vinegar
2 tablespoons water
2 tablespoons sugar
1 tablespoon dill weed
1 teaspoon mustard seed
salt and pepper to taste
1 large cucumber, thinly sliced

Directions

1. Mix vinegar, water, sugar and spices to make a marinade.

2. Pour over cucumbers.

3. Chill a few hours to allow marinade to flavor cucumbers.

Feel free to add red onion and/or olives to this summer dish. You can use the marinade for fresh green beans and garlic or three bean salad. Eileen taught my pre-natal aerobics class and was on my tennis team.

Oven Grilled Vegetables

1 red pepper
1 yellow pepper
1 orange pepper
½ onion
2 small zucchini
1 yellow squash
8 ounces mushrooms
¼ cup balsamic vinegar
1 tablespoon dried parsley
2 teaspoons basil
1 teaspoon cumin
2 teaspoons oregano
1 tablespoon garlic purée
¼ cup black olive tapenade

Directions

1. Cut all vegetables into bite size pieces and place in large bowl.
2. Cover with remaining ingredients.
3. Mix thoroughly and let vegetables marinate overnight, stir a few times.
4. Bake at 350°, uncovered in a 9X13" glass baking dish for 45 minutes.

Other seasonal vegetables can be used. If you have a vegetable basket, you can grill on your BBQ without losing the vegetables.

THE GUY SECTION

Can I have your attention please? I decided that I needed to write a section for guys only. Why, because so many men have issues with being "vegan," or "plant-based." It is almost like wearing pink. Some guys are okay with it, and others aren't.

I will get right to the point. There are reasons why men should be very concerned with what they eat. Especially as they get older. Have I got your attention yet? They haven't proven this yet, but I can recite anecdotal references to increased sexual performance. Now, I bet I have your attention. At fifteen to twenty dollars per pill, you can go to some pretty fancy plant-based restaurants.

Dr. Esselstyn has the best story. He talks about the patient that called him back after being on a plant-based diet for a while and said, "Dr. Esselstyn, I had a side effect of the diet." The doctor asked what was it and the patient said, "I raised the flag." Check out "vegan is the new Viagra": http://www.forksoverknives.com/fok-releases-raising-the-flag-with-a-vegan-diet-about-sexual-dysfunction/. Now that I have your attention, let me provide some recipes especially for you.

Nachos

In search of something with "crunch"?

- 1 cup cooked bulgur*
- 2 tablespoons Mexican seasoning
- 1 15 ounce can black beans, drained
- 1 can Rotel tomatoes, drained
- 8 corn tortillas, cut into triangles
  Cheese Sauce (recipe on next page)
- 1 tomato, chopped
- 1 avocado, chopped
- 3 green onions, sliced
  salsa as desired

Directions

1. Bring ⅓ cup dry bulgur and ⅔ cup water to a boil. Cover and simmer 10-20 minutes until bulgur is tender.
2. Mix bulgur, Mexican seasoning, black beans and Rotel tomatoes in a small bowl.
3. Bake corn tortilla triangles in a 425° oven until crisp (homemade chips).
4. Place homemade chips on pizza pan, layer with bulgur and bean mixture.
5. Top with spoonfuls of Cheese Sauce.
6. Heat in 350° oven about 20-30 minutes until hot.
7. Top with tomato, avocado and green onions.

Perfect appetizer for your next football party.

I brought this to a party and the man of the house swooped in on the nachos and ate with gusto. His comment, "If I didn't know who brought this, I would think it had meat in it."

*Try substituting quinoa for your gluten-free friends.

Cheese Sauce

1 large sweet potato, 2 cups diced
½ small onion, cut in large pieces
1 cup vegetable broth
4 tablespoons nutritional yeast
½ cup raw cashews

Directions

1. Boil sweet potato and onion in 1 cup of vegetable broth until tender.

2. Stir nutritional yeast and cashews into the potato onion mixture and blend until smooth with an immersion blender.

This recipe makes quite a bit of cheese sauce, more than what you would use for the nacho recipe. Use the leftovers as a sauce for vegetables or put a spoonful between two pieces of toast for a mock grilled cheese sandwich.

Parmesan Cheese

¼ cup raw cashews
2 tablespoons nutritional yeast
2 tablespoons hemp seed
¼ teaspoon salt
⅛ teaspoon garlic powder

Directions

1. Mix all ingredients in a coffee bean grinder.

2. Refrigerate in a small jar.

Use this whenever a recipe calls for nutritional yeast for an authentic Parmesan taste.

Rutabaga Fries

2 pounds rutabaga, peeled and cut into strips like fries
1 teaspoon olive oil, or less
  garlic powder
  cayenne pepper
  salt
  paprika
2 tablespoons Dijon mustard
2 teaspoons Sriracha chili sauce
1 tablespoon vinegar

Directions

1. Preheat oven to 425°.

2. Place oil into large plastic bag (gallon size) and put the rutabaga into the bag to coat. Try to evenly distribute oil on all surfaces of the fries (just squeeze them around).

3. Place parchment paper on baking sheet and spread rutabaga in a single layer.

4. Sprinkle with spices.

5. Bake 45 minutes until starting to brown.

6. Serve with dipping sauce made by combining Dijon mustard, Sriracha and vinegar.

For the most part, most of my recipes are made without added oils. Sometimes, fat is needed for the browning process. Believe me, you would not have liked the fries I made without oil. I have fond memories of rutabaga because my Uncle Eddie cooked it every Thanksgiving. "Uncle" is in his 90's.

Portobello Mushroom Steaks

3 tablespoons tamari
2 tablespoons balsamic vinegar
3 cloves garlic, minced
1 tablespoon ginger, minced
1 tablespoon brown sugar
4 large portobello mushrooms
   Zip Sauce, optional (recipe on next page)

Directions

1. Gently brush mushrooms and cut stem to be even with cap.

2. Place mushrooms smooth side down on a baking sheet.

3. Mix together remaining ingredients and spoon into caps, it is fine if some of the sauce gets out.

4. Marinate mushrooms at least 30 minutes.

5. Bake in 350° oven, for 30-45 minutes.

6. You can cook on the grill for 10 minutes on each side. Grill marks add to the eye appeal and make the omnivore happy.

7. Serve with Zip Sauce.

The grilling of animal products, especially fatty meats has come under fire (sorry, I had to put the pun in for my dad) as the char produced from the flame from grease flare-up is considered carcinogenic. Grilled vegetables are considered safe, and are quite delicious. When I went on a group camping trip to Lake Powell, I brought a virgin grill (one that never had any animal products on it), just for my vegetables. You certainly don't need to be this extreme!

Zip Sauce

2 ounces sherry
2 ounces water
1 tablespoon ground flax seed
1 tablespoon Dijon mustard
2 teaspoons Worcestershire sauce*
1 teaspoon rosemary
¼ teaspoon thyme
¼ teaspoon garlic powder
1 teaspoon parsley
1 teaspoon salt
½ teaspoon black pepper
¼ teaspoon ground cumin
⅛ teaspoon cayenne pepper
⅛ teaspoon white pepper

Directions

1. Place sherry, water, ground flax seed, Dijon mustard and Worcestershire sauce in a small saucepan and simmer 10 minutes over low heat.

2. Meanwhile, mix the herbs and spices, add to saucepan to blend flavors.

   Use as a "steak sauce" for portobello mushroom steaks.

This is a recipe from a healthy old guy from Detroit, Michigan that says grilled portobello mushrooms with Zip Sauce are every bit as good as a steak.

*If you are vegan, purchase vegan Worcestershire sauce.

Dirty Vegetables

1 white onion, coarse chopped
5 cups of root vegetables cut into cubes
½ cup orange juice
2 tablespoons balsamic vinegar
1 clove garlic, minced
   ground cayenne red pepper to taste
2 teaspoons real maple syrup

Directions

1. Fill a glass 9X13" baking dish with onion and root vegetables (beets* of all colors, sweet potatoes, carrots, purple potatoes, any vegetable that grows in the ground).

2. Mix together orange juice, vinegar, garlic, cayenne pepper and real maple syrup.

3. Drizzle mixture over the vegetables and toss to coat.

4. Cover with foil and bake at 350° for 45 minutes. Remove foil and continue to bake 15-30 minutes until tender and tasty.

The only way we can keep vegetables different is to demand different vegetables. Today I used golden, traditional red and candy stripe beets. If you think eating plant-based is boring, you need to expand your vegetable choices. The dirty truth, there are a lot more vegetables to eat than there are animals.

*You might want to wear gloves when cutting beets as they turn everything red (including your hands). I leave the peels on all vegetables to increase fiber.

1 cup tequila
1 cup triple sec
1 cup lime juice
1 small can frozen limeade
  ice

Directions

1. Blend well and pour over ice.

This recipe is "plant-based." As my friend Paul says: "My sister is on a plant-based diet: She has vodka (made with potatoes), cigarettes (made with leaves) and coffee (made with beans)." This brings up the point that not all plant-based foods are "healthy." This is a perfect example.

THE LAST COURSE

Let me leave you with just a few more tidbits. By now you have had a chance to sample the food, enjoy, and reap the benefits of eating a healthier diet. I hope you are walking down the path to better health. We all get to decide what we want to eat. It is important to respect the decisions others make about their dietary choices, just as we need to show respect for differing political or religious views. We are not here to judge or be judged. That being said, it is all right to encourage the people in your life to adopt a healthy lifestyle. After all, we want these people to be around for as long as we are and we want them to feel good while they are here. The last section contains some items to be used with MODERATION, things like quick breads, desserts and adult beverages. I didn't want anybody to think I was a saint. I am far from it.

This is the section where I need to tell you about sugar, salt and fat. I bet I don't need to tell you that these items can cause health problems. Sugar, salt and fat are considered inflammatory. In the grain section, I introduced the importance of fiber in your diet. It is important to make sure you have fiber with your sugar. Fiber helps temper the blood sugar response. How much sugar, salt and added oils you include in your diet is a personal choice that you must make based upon your health conditions and your dietary goals. If you start eating a prudent diet, your taste buds change.

Let's talk about alcohol. Living in Aspen has exposed me to the negative effects of alcohol.

Yes, we have science that proves moderate alcohol intake is good for us. Remember, I said earlier that people can prove anything they want. You have probably heard about the benefits of red wine. There is a compound in red wine, resveratrol, that has been studied with regard to heart disease. Still, most doctors are not going to recommend drinking. You can get resveratrol from red grapes, it just isn't as much fun. There is also a negative association between alcohol intake and cancer. This is where moderation comes in. You have to love a word like moderation, it is so subjective. This is where you get to decide how much risk you want to take. What is the balance between pleasure and health?

One last story. I was helping in my son's first grade class. The kids were working in small groups, the teacher was across the room from me. I overheard my son say, "My mom likes to drink a lot." The teacher obviously heard this too, as she raised her eyebrows to me. He finished his sentence, "Her favorite drink is water." By now you know that I am passionately plant-based. I believe eating this way is good for our health, the animals and our environment.

"In a gentle way, you can shake up the world"
—Mahatma Gandhi

Banana Blueberry Bread

Pumpkin Pie

Crust:

- 1 cup walnuts
- 9 Medjool dates, pitted
- pinch salt

Filling:

- ½ cup granulated sugar
- 1 teaspoon cinnamon
- ½ teaspoon salt
- ¼ teaspoon cloves
- 2 tablespoons chia seeds
- 1 cup unsweetened almond milk
- ½ ripe avocado
- 1 teaspoon vanilla
- 1 inch piece fresh ginger, peeled and cut (or 1/2 teaspoon ground ginger)
- 1 15 ounce can pumpkin

Directions

1. To make crust, place walnuts in a small food processor and chop.
2. Add dates 2 at a time mixing to make a paste.
3. Add salt and mix.
4. Press into 9" pie pan and bake at 425° for 7-10 minutes.
5. Meanwhile make the filling.
6. In a large heavy duty blender mix sugar, cinnamon, salt, cloves, chia seeds, almond milk, avocado, vanilla, fresh ginger and canned pumpkin.
7. Pour filling into walnut and date crust.
8. Bake at 425° for 15 minutes.
9. Turn down heat to 350° and bake 40 minutes longer.
10. Serve room temperature the first day or cold from the refrigerator.

Chia seeds are high in the plant form of omega-3 fatty acid. Chia seeds, in this recipe, are the egg substitute and help the pie form a pudding-like consistency.

Creamy Chocolate Pudding

1½ cups lite unflavored soy milk
⅓ cup pure maple syrup
¼ cup cocoa powder
3 tablespoons cornstarch
¼ teaspoon vanilla extract

Directions

1. Whisk soy milk, maple syrup, cocoa powder and cornstarch together in a medium saucepan.

2. Cook over medium heat, stirring constantly until thickened.

3. Stir in vanilla and pour into individual serving dishes.

4. Cool in refrigerator for 2 hours.

There is something about chocolate. Other than wine, it is the thing most people are afraid they will have to give up when going plant-based. Thankfully you don't have to give up either!

Chocolate Cake

1¼ cups 100% whole wheat pastry flour
1 cup sugar
⅓ cup cocoa
1 teaspoon baking soda
½ teaspoon salt
1 cup warm water
1 teaspoon vanilla extract
½ cup applesauce
1 teaspoon vinegar

Directions

1. Mix ingredients together and pour in lightly oiled 9X9" pan.

2. Bake at 350° for 30 minutes.

3. For simple frosting, take your favorite chocolate bar and break a few pieces on top of warm cake. Spread with a knife as the chocolate melts. (Optional, as it adds fat.)

This cake is just too delicious to be fat-free. I made this cake for my high school friend, Sue. When she heard I was making her birthday cake, she was less than thrilled. Afterwards, she said it was the best chocolate cake ever.

Zucchini Bread

4 tablespoons ground flax seed
3 tablespoons water
2 cups sugar
1 cup applesauce
2 cups zucchini, grated
1 tablespoon vanilla
3 cups 100% whole wheat pastry flour
1 teaspoon salt
¼ teaspoon baking powder
1 teaspoon baking soda
1 tablespoon cinnamon
1 cup walnuts, chopped

Directions

1. Mix ground flax seed with water and set aside (this is your egg substitute).
2. Combine remaining ingredients and stir in flax seed mixture.
3. Pour into 2 non-stick loaf pans and bake at 350° for 1 hour.

Great way to use those giant zucchini and hide a serving of vegetable in your dessert. Try to get 8 servings of vegetables per day.

Gingerbread

1¼ cups 100% whole wheat flour
2 teaspoons baking powder
1 teaspoon baking soda
2 teaspoons cinnamon
¼ teaspoon ground cloves
½ teaspoon salt
¾ cup applesauce
½ cup unsulfured blackstrap molasses
⅔ cup real maple syrup
¾ cup soy or almond milk
1 tablespoon orange zest
2 tablespoons minced ginger

Directions

1. Preheat oven to 325°.
2. Mix together dry ingredients.
3. In a separate bowl combine liquid ingredients.
4. Mix dry and liquid ingredients together.
5. Pour into a lightly greased 9X13" baking dish.
6. Bake 50 minutes.
7. Cool slightly before serving.

The Bar

3 cups oatmeal, dry
1½ cups brown rice flour*
½ cup hemp seed
3 tablespoons ground flax seed
2 teaspoons cinnamon
¼ teaspoon nutmeg
½ teaspoon baking soda
½ teaspoon salt
½ cup orange juice
1 teaspoon vanilla
½ cup applesauce
½ cup real maple syrup
½ cup pumpkin seeds
½ cup sunflower seeds
1½ cups dried fruit, chopped

Directions

1. Mix together dry ingredients.
2. Mix together liquid ingredients and stir into dry.
3. Fold in seeds and dried fruit.
4. Press into a 9X13" baking pan lined with parchment paper.
5. Bake at 350° for 30 minutes until golden brown.

Cut into 10 bars, each bar provides approximately 15 grams of protein. Perfect for breakfast or sports bar.

*If you don't have brown rice flour, you can use 100% whole wheat.

Pumpkin Bread

1¾ cups 100% whole wheat pastry flour
1 cup brown sugar
1 teaspoon baking soda
½ teaspoon baking powder
½ teaspoon salt
1 teaspoon cinnamon
½ teaspoon nutmeg
½ teaspoon allspice
¼ teaspoon cloves
1 15 ounce can pumpkin
½ cup applesauce
3 tablespoons real maple syrup
3 tablespoons water
1 teaspoon white vinegar
½ cup pumpkin seeds

Directions

1. Preheat oven to 350°.
2. In a large bowl, mix together all dry ingredients.
3. Add pumpkin, applesauce, syrup, water and vinegar.
4. Stir in pumpkin seeds.
5. Pour into greased and floured loaf pan and bake 45-50 minutes.

Pumpkin is high in fiber and Vitamin A. Although this bread is not low in sugar, the fiber in both the pumpkin and the whole wheat flour helps control your body's reaction to it.

Banana Blueberry Bread

½ cup applesauce
½ cup sugar
1½ cups 100% whole wheat flour
½ teaspoon baking soda
1½ teaspoons baking powder
½ teaspoon salt
½ cup soy milk
1 teaspoon vanilla
1 teaspoon white vinegar
2 mashed bananas
¾ cup blueberries
½ cup walnuts, chopped

Directions

1. Mix applesauce and sugar.
2. Add flour, baking soda, baking powder, salt and mix.
3. Stir in soy milk, vanilla and vinegar.
4. Add bananas, blueberries and walnuts.
5. Bake in loaf pan, 350° for 50 minutes.

Always a "hit" at the tennis match pot-luck. A great dessert or an on-the-go breakfast. Moist and delicious, nobody will know it is healthy!

Peach Crisp

8 fresh peaches, sliced
1 cup rolled oats
¼ cup 100% whole wheat flour
½ cup pecans, chopped
½ cup brown sugar
½ teaspoon salt
2 tablespoons lemon juice

Directions

1. Lightly grease 8X8" baking pan.

2. Line with sliced peaches.

3. In small bowl combine remaining ingredients and spread over peaches.

4. Bake at 350° for 45-60 minutes.

My friend Pam lives on the Colorado River and has a peach tree in her yard. After floating the river, I left with more ripe peaches than I could possibly eat. Decadent for breakfast or a perfect summer dessert.

Black Bean Brownies

When asked "what is in your brownie?" my silence created rumor of "magic brownies." I guess they are magically healthy!

    1 15 ounce can black beans, drained and rinsed
    1 cup water
 1½ cups 100% whole wheat flour
    1 teaspoon salt
    1 teaspoon baking powder
 1¾ cups sugar
 1¼ cups cocoa powder
   ¼ teaspoon mace (optional)
    2 teaspoons cinnamon
       pinch cayenne pepper
    1 teaspoon vanilla
 1½ cups walnut pieces
   ½ cup chocolate chips

Directions

1. Preheat oven to 350°.
2. In food processor blend black beans with water until smooth.
3. Combine all dry ingredients.
4. With mixer on low, add black bean purée and vanilla to dry ingredients, and mix thoroughly.
5. Add nuts and chocolate chips (use carob chips to make them totally vegan), mix to combine.
6. Pour batter into 9X13" (nonstick or lightly greased) baking pan.
7. Bake 45 minutes, do not overcook. Edges will just start to pull away from the pan.

Pomegranate Martini

½ cup pomegranate seeds
5 ounces vodka
5 ounces pomegranate juice
½ lime
1 cup crushed ice

Directions

1. Muddle seeds in martini shaker.
2. Add vodka, pomegranate juice and the juice of lime.
3. Add crushed ice.
4. Shake and strain into martini glasses.
5. Garnish with a few pomegranate seeds.

If you are a true vegan, you might want to search this site: http://www.barnivore.com/.
Not all alcoholic beverages are vegan friendly.

Chocolate Martini

1 ounce Dorda chocolate liqueur
1 ounce chocolate infused vodka
1 ounce creme de cacao
    shaved ice

Directions

1. Place all ingredients into martini shaker.
2. Shake and serve in chocolate dipped martini glasses.

I melt chocolate chips on a plate in the microwave and swirl the martini glass around to coat. Make these ahead so the chocolate has time to cool.

This is NOT healthy, NOT vegan, but my evil twin made me put in the recipe.

APPENDIX AND FOOD GLOSSARY

Gourmet Garden
Although most of these
are not vegan (they contain
whey) they are a time saver
and I love having the cilantro
in my refrigerator.

Bragg Liquid Aminos
I like the spray bottle
to spritz things.

Sriracha Hot
Chili Sauce
This is hot!

Silken Tofu
Shelf stable, great for
softer things like sauces
and puddings.

Tahini
Or, make your own
https://www.youtube.com/
watch?v=a8FNouH7c5I

Nutritional Yeast
Good source of B12
(necessary for vegan diet).

Better Than Bouillon
Easy vegetable broth–
make just what you need.

Tamari
I buy the low sodium organic.

Trocomare

Spicy Salt Blend

**Santa Cruz Organic
Lime and Lemon Juice**

Sun Dried Tomatoes

(no added oil)

**Simply
Organic Sweet
Basil Pesto**

Ginger People

Ginger Juice

Dr. Kracker

My favorite cracker.

Dave's Killer Bread

Although I heard rumor Dave was back in jail, he still has a good high fiber bread.

Pomì Tomatoes

These are tomatoes and just tomatoes.

Ancient Harvest Quinoa in the Box

This is pre-washed. Most quinoa must be washed prior to use to remove a bitter naturally occurring chemical (saponin).

Muir Glen Canned Tomatoes

These have a little sodium (salt) added.

Tinkyada Brown Rice Pasta

This is higher in fiber and gluten free.

365 Bread Crumbs

PANTRY

Canned or shelf stable box beans (black, garbanzo, pinto, white)*

Canned tomato products (crushed, diced, marinara, paste)*

Dried lentils and split peas

Pasta

Quinoa

Barley

Oats

Rice (brown, black, wild)

Dried fruits (cherries, cranberries, blueberries, apricots, dates)

Applesauce in 4 ounce cups (fat substitute)

Non-dairy unsweetened milk (soy, rice, almond or hemp)

Lite coconut milk

Raw nuts (cashews, walnuts, pecans, almonds, pistachios, pine)

Seeds (pumpkin, sunflower, hemp, flax)

Vinegar (apple cider, white, balsamic, red wine)

Lemon and lime juice

Nut butters (peanut, almond, tahini)

Dijon mustard

Vegan Worcestershire sauce

Sweeteners (sugar, brown sugar, molasses, maple syrup)

Sriracha hot chili sauce

Salsa

Braggs Liquid Aminos spray

Low Sodium Tamari (use instead of soy sauce)

Vegetarian broth (cubes, boxed, canned or jar)*

Herbs and spices in small quantities to keep fresh

Onions, potatoes and garlic

Low sodium recommended

REFRIGERATOR AND FREEZER

Vegetables
(seasonal fresh and frozen)
Fruits
(seasonal fresh and frozen juices)

 Sandy, a registered dietitian nutritionist and long-time vegetarian, is passionate about the value of a plant-based lifestyle. This cookbook, which includes some of her personal bests as well as requested favorites from family and friends, are all simple to prepare yet delicious to eat. In addition to recipes, Sandy's scientific background enables her to share relevant nutritional information.

A clinical dietitian at Aspen Valley Hospital for more than 30 years, Sandy has positively influenced her own hospital's food service. Sandy and team have developed vegan options for AVH staff and patients, resulting in the hospital receiving special recognition for the best hospital food in the nation.

Outside the hospital, Sandy looks for new ways to share her healthy eating practices with family, friends and her community. She developed and teaches a class called "Leaning Toward a Plant-Based Diet." She regularly teaches healthy cooking classes. These classes, along with Aspen Meatless Monday events, are eagerly anticipated and well attended by members of the community.

Always interested in food and cooking, Sandy earned a Bachelors of Science degree in Dietetics from Purdue University. Immediately after graduation, she headed west to Colorado to pursue her love of healthy cooking, eating and living. When not sharing the benefits of a plant-based diet, Sandy loves to ski and spend time outdoors. She hopes her enthusiasm for plant-based nutrition will resonate with you and inspire you to move towards a healthier lifestyle.

CPSIA information can be obtained
at www.ICGtesting.com
Printed in the USA
FSOW04n0833171116
27500FS